The
Recovery Formula

An Addict's Guide to getting Clean and Sober
Forever

by Beth Burgess

First published in the UK in 2012

Published by Eightball Publishing

ISBN 978-0-9573217-0-0

About the Book

The Recovery Formula is an essential guide for anyone who is addicted to alcohol or drugs and is ready to do something about it. Having struggled as a serial relapser before achieving her own recovery, Beth Burgess shares the universal lessons she has learnt about what really works and what doesn't when it comes to getting clean and sober.

The book will help you to understand your problem, to make decisions about treatment, to avoid relapse and to set yourself up for success from the start.

Your recovery starts here.

About the Author

Beth Burgess is a Life and Recovery Coach and the founder of Sort My Life Solutions (Smyls). She provides private coaching, consulting, workshops and training.

Her missions include helping as many people as possible to achieve an amazing recovery, and ending the stigma shown towards people with addiction problems.

Visit Beth at www.smyls.co.uk or www.bethburgess.co.uk

To ma and dad -
I can't even count the reasons why.

Contents

Dare to reach out your hand into the darkness, to pull another hand into the light.

- Norman B. Rice

Foreword

by Professor David Clark, Director of Wired In To Recovery

Over the years I've worked in this field, I have heard from many people with substance use problems who have struggled to understand their addiction. They had a strong desire to give up using drugs, or to stop drinking, but had no idea how to go about it. They had tried to stop using or drinking on numerous occasions, but they kept on relapsing.

Even though they had been in and out of treatment, this had not given them a real understanding of what it takes to recover from addiction. They had become confused and frustrated by their lack of progress (and the failure of treatment services to help them). They had lost confidence and self-belief. Their self-esteem had sometimes become so damaged that they had contemplated suicide, as the only way out of their problems.

Many of these people also spoke of the positive impact that coming into contact with recovering, or recovered people, had on their lives, and of how this had been fundamental to their recovery. They described how they related positively to these recovering people, role models who spoke the same language, and shared similar experiences, thoughts and feelings. These role models showed both that recovery is possible and that there are many pathways to recovery. They were people who could be trusted, and who understood the nature of a life of addiction.

Role models are so very important because recovery is something that comes from the person. It is not something given to a person by a treatment service or practitioner. The person with the substance use problem does the work. But recovery is also a social process. People learn from other people about the nature of their problem (addiction), the solution (recovery), and what they have to do to take the journey to recovery.

Given all of this, it is surprising that there are so few widely-circulated recovery guidebooks written by people who are in recovery. Most of the books on substance use problems focus on addiction, rather than becoming well. Many books are too academic. What people who want to overcome their addiction need is a simple book that provides information about the fundamental building blocks of recovery. A book to which they can relate.

That is exactly what Beth Burgess has done in her wonderfully refreshing book *The Recovery Formula*. Beth talks about the essential elements underlying recovery in a beautifully accessible way. A way that comes from experience - and will be easy to relate to for people who want to recover from a substance use problem. She describes the sorts of things she attempted when trying to overcome her own drinking problems, some of which helped her move towards recovery, others which did little, or in fact impeded progress. Beth's description of her past shows how easy it is for an uninformed person to stumble from one unhelpful tactic to another.

Beth's book describes a framework comprising four key building blocks to recovery. She tells people they must: *Get Honest, Get Held, Get Committed and Get Replacements.* Beth talks about key principles that have been shown to facilitate recovery. These principles are known to play a significant role in successful treatment approaches, mutual aid and self-help approaches.

The Recovery Formula succeeds because it provides people in need of help with a solid, proven framework in an easy-to-understand way. Beth speaks as a person who has "been there", explaining the pitfalls, as well as helpful strategies, allowing the reader to gain a firm footing on the path to recovery, rather than stumble around and get caught in the common traps that await the unwary. The book empowers the reader with information that will directly help their recovery, as well as help them to understand the resources in their community that will also facilitate their recovery.

What is also brilliant about this book is that it embodies what recovery is about, and what recovering addicts can achieve. Recovery is not just about stopping the use of substances. It is about getting your whole life back, developing new networks, new interests and moving forward. As Beth points out, recovery is about getting better physically, mentally and emotionally - and creating a life that you enjoy and of which you are proud.

Recovery is also about connecting with other people. It is about helping other people, as so beautifully illustrated by Beth, both in relation to her book and her role as a Recovery Coach.

There is a blossoming Recovery Movement, which is engaging people who want to recover from addiction and those who are already on their journey. This rapidly growing Recovery Movement is inspiring hope, showing how people find recovery, and providing the opportunity for people to engage in mutual support. People are starting to celebrate and share their recoveries more publicly, by telling their stories, blogging on our online recovery community *Wired In To Recovery*, participating in Recovery Walks, engaging in Conversation Cafes, and setting up Recovery Cafes.

Now we have a new book about recovery, one which I recommend strongly. I am sure you will benefit from reading this book. I hope you will help others benefit as well. You can do this by telling other people about the book.

Remember, Recovery is Contagious. Let's make *The Recovery Formula* contagious.

*****

David Clark is Founder and Director of Wired In, an Emeritus Professor of Psychology, and a dedicated addiction recovery advocate. He is currently writing a book and researching a documentary on Recovery Stories.

Wired In is a unique grass-roots initiative that was developed to empower people to tackle drug and alcohol use problems, and to make society more understanding of people affected by substance use problems. The Wired In online recovery community (www.wiredintorecovery.org) provides information and tools to facilitate recovery, and an empathic environment where people help each other to better their lives.

Introduction

If you have come to a point in your life where you realise that you are hopelessly addicted to alcohol or drugs, this book is here to help. There is hope, and people do recover from addictions and go on to lead wonderful lives.

I assume that if you are reading this book you have decided you want to recover from your addiction – or you are at least considering your options. But the problem is there are so many treatments and services out there. How do you know what will be the best fit for you?

Or maybe you believe that simply stopping taking drugs or drinking will be the answer to your prayers and you will magically be better after putting them down. Sadly that is not the case. There is no point in simply stopping drinking or taking drugs – you need to take certain critical steps that are essential to sobriety and recovery.

We have generally been led to believe that addiction is an overwhelming illness that is difficult to beat. We hear about people going in and out of rehabs, hospitals and even prisons and mental institutions, before they finally get clean and sober for good. This is why I have put together this book. There seems to be no other guide out there which lays out a Formula for you, teaching you how to get clean and sober in a simple way. No-one has picked out all the elements of treatment and found out just why they work.

And that is why addicts can spend years of their lives going from pillar to post, trying one treatment after another, and even trying the same treatments over and over again to no avail. It is not necessarily that the treatments are wrong or that they don't work, but they are only part of the picture. It is all very well to go to Relapse Prevention groups, AA, rehab or counselling, but if you don't understand the fundamental building blocks of recovery, then you haven't got the whole solution. How can you be expected to get better if you don't really know what you're doing?

It is said that individuals need different treatments to stay sober. What may work for one person may not work for another. While this is partly true, I believe that the particular elements that all successful treatments have can be broken down into a pattern of steps, or a framework, that anyone can use to recover. There are certain things that make treatments successful – and I have picked out the essential pieces and devised a Formula that anyone can follow to get, and stay, sober.

Attempting to end your addiction without implementing this Formula, is at best a game of chance, and at worst, pointless and horribly painful. I know that because I am an alcoholic and I did recovery all wrong the first time around and am lucky to have survived to tell the tale. I have written this book so that you do not have to make the same mistakes that I did. You will be more likely to succeed at the treatments and services available to you when you understand the value of them, which ones might suit you best, and how they can help you to follow the Formula for a lasting recovery.

This book is here to give you the solution if you want to get clean and sober and stay that way forever. I should point out that if the words 'sober forever' are making you slightly unnerved, try to think of it in these terms. Do you want to be free of your addiction forever? Do you want to be liberated from its horrible grasp on your life so that you can be free and happy forever? If the answer to that is "yes", then this book is for you.

I have no agenda with this book other than to help you get well. I, personally, know what a heartbreakingly difficult cross addiction is to bear. I also know how painful it is to stop drinking but not take steps towards recovery. I do not care what your personal preferences for treatment are – all I want you to do is follow this Formula, stay sober and start working towards recovery. The rest is up to you.

The Formula

The great thing about my Recovery Formula is that it is simple to follow and applies to everyone. I believe that, because people are individuals, there may not be a treatment system that fits everyone. However, this is the beauty of the Recovery Formula. If you follow the Formula you can individualise your own treatment plan.

As long as you stick to the basic steps, you have the freedom to choose the way in which you implement it.

The Formula is designed to suit anyone who is trying to stop taking drugs or drinking and wants to take their first steps towards sobriety and, ultimately, recovery. What you need in early sobriety is different from what you need to fully recover. Early sobriety is fraught with difficulties and temptations to use drink or drugs that are not as apparent later on in recovery. But you can not recover without sobriety first, so this framework is designed to set you up so you are able to sustain sobriety and become ready to recover.

I have divided the Formula into four parts to make it easy for you to follow. In each part I will explain all the elements of it, so you can understand why it works and how to implement it.

The first two parts of the Formula are essential to keep you sober early on so that you are able to move on to the final two steps that will help you start to recover. You can only work on your recovery when you are clean and sober. But, being clean and sober is difficult when you haven't recovered, and so you really have to give your recovery your all and apply maximum commitment. I promise you, if you commit yourself, the end result will be worth it. When it feels difficult early on, always keep the end goal in mind – being happy, recovered and free.

Throughout this book, I will share my own experiences with you, what I have learnt on my journey to recovery, some of the lessons I learnt the hard way, and of course the four parts of the Formula so that you can follow them for yourself.

I am not going to tell you that recovery is easy, because of course it's not, but then nothing worth having is easy. However, what I will say is that recovery can be simple if you just follow my Recovery Formula.

So let's start with the first part...

Part One

Get Real

The first part of the Recovery Formula involves getting real about your problem, stopping the justifications and excuses and recognising, honestly, the part that drink or drugs is playing in your life.

Your alcohol or drug problem is bigger than you. It's a massive all-encompassing problem that affects every area of your life. If you don't believe that's true then you just haven't been addicted long enough yet.

You may have had enough money or people enabling you to keep pushing you through without any external damage so far, or you may just have been so determined to keep your addiction going that you've escaped for the moment without any major disasters. This is, in some ways, very fortunate for you, but in other ways it means that you may be deluded as to the nature of addiction.

But rest assured, if you have a problem with feeling compelled to use drugs or alcohol, unless you stop, the addiction monster will overtake your life sooner or later. I know because I've been there. And so have many, many other people.

If you have ever felt compelled to use drink or drugs against your will, or found that once you start you can not stop, or you keep swearing off substances only to return to them again and again, addiction has got you.

Have you ever acted irrationally and insanely around your substance of choice? Like knowing you can not have just a little in the cold light of day, but in the moment before using being absolutely convinced that this time it will be different? Do you lie to yourself as much as you do to others about your using? Can you find any excuse, big or small, to start using again? Have you ever found yourself at the off licence or your dealers when you were absolutely committed to not picking up that day? Have you ever spent the day locked in the house or going on a really long walk, because you knew if you didn't take drastic action you would use? Have you ever felt that feeling of dread that no matter what you try to do today to stop yourself, you will use anyway? Have you ever stopped using for any length of time and then when you returned to your substance, things were even worse than before?

These are all signs that you have come to a place of no return with your addiction. There is no getting out of it or moderating now. There is only the choice between being trapped forever – or abstinence and recovery. I explain the above because I was utterly confused as to the nature of my own problem and how to solve it. There were many things I did not realise, even when I had admitted I was an addict and knew I had to stop. There were fallacies I believed and things I told myself because I did not fully understand the nature of the problem.

I am going to address these here so that you can be armed with knowledge and understanding of your own problem.

What doesn't work

So first, let us be very clear on what doesn't work when it comes to recovering from alcohol or drug addiction. It is important to go through this information so that you can recognise if you may be fooling yourself about stopping, or setting yourself up for failure.

A lot of us fall into certain traps when we decide to sort out our drinking or drugging and these jeopardise both our sobriety, and in turn, any chance of recovery; so it is very important to be aware of them.

Controlled Using

Some people believe that they would be alright if they could just curb their addiction a bit, and this might mean controlling their drinking or taking fewer drugs. Maybe puffing instead of snorting, or perhaps smoking rather than injecting. I went down that route myself for a while, until I realised that the alcohol was firmly in control and I could only count the number of times I was 'victorious' over it on the fingers of one hand. There were a few times when I managed to drink and it wasn't that bad, or I didn't go massively overboard, but trying to control my use was an unpleasant experience overall.

I can laugh when I look back at it now, as I desperately tried to control my drinking. It was such a big effort and ultimately a waste of time. I had several methods, which I was convinced were going to be my saving grace, but they all failed me one by one.

First I made rules for myself about when I was allowed to drink, and I told myself, for example, that I would only drink in company. Of course, that meant I saw my friends a lot more in the beginning – but I was still drinking almost as much as before, and the consequences were often bigger because I got other people involved. Then I decided that I would only drink down the pub – of course that led to me swiftly downing pints and following up with secret triple Cognacs whenever I went to the bar. It was 'my round' surprisingly often. Again, I got into more trouble that way than I had when I was drinking at home.

So then I decided to scrap the 'when and where', and chose only to drink after a certain time of day. Cue binge drinking at 5pm on weekdays and then again at noon on the weekends when I told myself I was being a bit hard on myself with this new rule!

The next genius idea I came up with was buying some measuring cups like those you see in the pub or bar. I'd limit myself to a certain number of 'measures' of whisky every day. Of course, when I saw the size of the measly things I quickly changed my allowances, and of course, more often than not, it was one measure for the glass and three for me straight out of the bottle. I even bought a decanter once, as if that would add a touch of normality and middle class-ness to my drinking. It didn't of course, as I'm sure you concluded before I even told you.

The final thing I tried was switching to 'weaker' drinks. I decided that it was the whisky that was making me particularly unpleasant and so I swore off that. And then later on I decided to ditch all the spirits when they seemed to be making me as bad as the whisky. So I downgraded to lager – not that really weak stuff, mind. It had to be premium. And I have never felt so dissatisfied with my drinking in my life. I found it was like drinking water.

Disappointed with my choice, I briefly flirted with alco-pops, until I discovered that they were making me fat rather than drunk. And so I moved up to wine. Now I hated wine really. I found the white stuff too sweet and the red stuff too vinegary. But I was an alcoholic and so I convinced myself to like it for the sake of my 'controlled drinking'. I even managed to pick myself a 'favourite' wine, as if that would help. I realise now that I only liked it because it packed a stronger punch than the others and tasted less like a 'pretend' drink. But the hangovers I got from wine were horrendous. And I was putting weight on again. So there was nothing for it but to go back to spirits. And so I was back to where I started - and probably worse than before.

The overwhelming difficulty I had when trying any form of controlled drinking was that it was such an effort. Firstly whenever you take that first drink, your inhibitions are lowered and you're much more likely to say "To hell with it" and settle down for a good session.

But the mental torture was the biggest problem for me. Every time I told myself I would only have three drinks, I was pining and itching for a fourth. I would get moody and frustrated if I had to wait to have a drink, or if I had reached my 'limit' for the day. And then, it struck me; I didn't want to control my drinking at all. I just wanted to stop having the problems that drinking was causing. What I really wanted was to be an utter booze-hound and get away with it! I wanted to drink until oblivion, how much I wanted, whenever I wanted it, and have no consequences to deal with.

Sadly, my dream would never be realised. It is just not possible to do that. You may manage it for some amount of time. In fact I had already done that. I was one of those functioning alcoholics for quite a while. But there is no way of sustaining that lifestyle without losing your physical or mental health, or both. Keith Richards is the only example I can think of who has ever achieved this ridiculous dream, and that's only because he has enough money to pay for an entire blood transfusion whenever his body has had enough. So unless you have more money than sense, give up your dreams of consequence-less drinking and decide to take real responsibility for your destiny by stopping drinking and drugging altogether.

Bargains

I remember when I first stopped drinking, I made a deal with my parents. I said, "OK, I promise I will be sober, unless..." And then I listed a number of likely scenarios that I 'knew' I would not be able to stay sober for.

Horrifyingly, I told my own parents that in the event of either of their deaths, I could not promise that I would stay sober. They smiled understandingly as I went on to list a number of additional deaths (including those of my friends, family and my pet cat) that I could not promise to stay sober for. And there I was, having already told myself I would relapse if anyone died.

Of course, my parents, bless them, and everyone else on my 'relapse/death' list, are still very much alive – and I eventually relapsed over something much more trivial in the grand scheme of things. But then, I had already told myself I would relapse. I had given myself permission to, and I had set myself up to fail.

The thing is, although I was very serious about my *desire* to stop drinking, there was a part of me that did not believe I could cope with being sober in such difficult circumstances.

Of course, I had to stop making bargains and be prepared to learn to cope if I was ever going to achieve long-term sobriety. If you think about it, most of us have a lot of people in our lives, and we can not place conditions on our sobriety, relating to them or anything else. People die and that's a part of life. Bad things happen – we can not jeopardise our recovery by making excuses based on those sorts of circumstances.

The way I see it now, I will be honouring my parents' memory by being sober when the painful day comes, as it is bound to do. Even if I spend a week, or a month, or a year feeling that pain, I will do so sober, and that's what they would have wanted me to do.

And this goes for all circumstances in life. You will never be able to control everything that happens to you in life. You can set yourself up for success and start making the right choices, but nothing can protect you from the hands of fate. Upsetting things happen sometimes, and we can not throw away our sobriety, just because something is painful.

The way that I have come to see my sobriety, is that I would rather die than jeopardise it. I must consider it as the most important thing in the world to me, because without it, I have nothing else. I have to put my sobriety above all other things. And that is not to say that I think about it all day or night – I don't. I get on with my life in a normal way and I don't let my addiction rule my life. But I would never, ever do anything that would put my sobriety at risk, including bargaining, because it is just too precious. I know my loved ones are fully supportive in that.

Addiction, sadly, is an illness just like any other. It does not give us time off to go a funeral, nor to celebrate a wedding or a birthday. Does diabetes or cancer ease off if you need a break? Can you stop taking insulin and eat a big slice of cake just because it's a celebration? No; and the same goes for addiction. There is no respite; there are no days off when you can have a few drinks or drugs – abstinence is something you have to commit to, no matter what you are going through in terms of life events.

The thing I have to remember is that pain may be horrible and unpleasant, but it will not kill me and does not spell the end of my life – sadly I can't put drinking or drugging in that same category. My addiction came very close to killing me, and I am certain that if I went down that route again, it would not hesitate to finish the job.

Short-term Fixes

You may well have got to the stage where you quite simply have to stop drinking or taking drugs, because it is having a devastating effect on your life. So why not just take a break from the drink or the drugs? Or make some changes and then maybe see if you want to go back to it afterwards?

Let me just tell you – an addiction is for life. You may well wish to find that out for yourself in the form of a mind-bendingly bad relapse. Or you could just take my word for it and save yourself a lot of pain.

Some of us may fall into the trap of believing that our addiction is a temporary condition, something brought on by circumstances or problems. Now that may be the case if you've had a very temporary setback. I have heard of people going through stressful periods, drinking a bit too much and then returning to normal drinking once their stress levels have returned to normal. Some people may have suffered a bereavement, or a divorce, or some other setback, with which drink or recreational drug use seemed a reasonable way to cope. I don't think it's a reasonable way to cope, by the way; you're better off just dealing with your feelings. But some people turn to it just the same. And I'm not saying they are addicts. If you've found that once that period of your life is over, you can return to sociable drinking, then good for you. I doubt you need to read this book.

But for some of us, even if we pick up the drink or drugs to deal with a specific situation, thinking that it will be a short-term fix, we find that we can *not* return to normal drinking - sometimes to our surprise and bewilderment. If you identified with any of the scenarios at the beginning of this section, then this almost certainly applies to you. There is nothing shameful or weak-willed attached to this inability to control your intake. It is simply because you are an addict, like me.

I'll tell you a bit about my own story. I almost became an alcoholic on purpose. That sounds quite strange, but when I started drinking all day, every day I knew exactly what I was doing and had no intentions of stopping. You see, I started drinking alcoholically because I had an anxiety disorder. It started off with being afraid to eat in front of people and progressed to me being scared to go outside. So when I first started drinking throughout the day, I was using it purely as a way of coping with the constant fear I felt. And it worked amazingly well for a few years, although the drinking was getting me into trouble and upsetting my friends and family. And after some time, it really started taking a toll on my physical health.

Throughout my years as a 'voluntary' alcoholic, I did try all sorts of things to deal with my anxiety disorder. Eventually I came across a cure that took just ninety minutes and I haven't been afraid to go outside ever since. It was an amazing day, not just in terms of the fact that I now felt no fear in the course of trying to function, but because I also thought that it meant I would return to drinking like everyone else. That was a double cause for celebration. The way I saw it, the sole reason for my unreasonable drinking was gone, and therefore I did not need to drink like an alcoholic any longer.

So off I would go down the pub with my friends, skipping down the street cheerfully, now that I was no longer afraid of the outside world. And yet I would wake up the next day, remembering little of the night before, or how I got home, and reeking of booze. Dismissing this as my brain not quite getting used to the fact that I didn't need to be an alcoholic any more, I tried and tried again to drink like any other sociable person. I was absolutely astounded that it didn't seem to be working. Logically, I should just be knocking back a few beers and having a laugh like my friends. But instead I was drinking until I blacked out and doing the same daft things I always did when drinking. I drank more than most of my mates put together and ended up in situations where I was out of control.

Being a rational person most of the time, it didn't make sense to me at all, and I refused for a long time to accept that this was it; I just was an alcoholic now and there was nothing I could do to change that. But I did have to accept it in the end, because the overwhelming evidence showed me that no matter why I started drinking, *now* I could not stop, even when I desperately wanted to.

Since I have been sober, I have looked back at the early part of my life and wondered if some of the signs showed that I was always likely to become a problematic drinker, even if I had never developed my anxiety disorder.

The symptoms of my anxiety disorder started to emerge very strongly at around the age of seventeen. By eighteen, I was drinking every day. And by nineteen, I was already physically dependent and a full-blown addict. But what about my drinking before the core problem really began?

Well, looking back on it, I have to admit that I probably wasn't ever that much of a normal drinker after all. When I was fourteen years old, I started going down the local graveyard with my friends and getting drunk and taking drugs every weekend. Now I'm not sure whether that is a totally normal thing to do as a kid or not. I certainly had friends that were not doing anything of the sort – they were listening to *Take That* and hanging around the local shopping centre, or getting involved in sports or youth clubs. But there were some of us who went out drinking and I know that not all of them have turned into addicts.

But when I look back on it, I was the only kid who never

really seemed to get sick off alcohol. While most of my mates would end up vomiting in a bush somewhere after drinking too many alco-pops, I would get into fights or do inappropriate things, but I hardly ever became physically sick. In fact, I can only recall two incidents during my childhood drinking when I actually vomited as a result of drinking too much. And it wasn't that I was drinking less than my peers. I wasn't. In fact I was on the cider and the lager while they played around with the alco-pops. But it seemed that my body was rather fond of the alcohol in a way that others' were not. And then, when I got a little older, and started venturing into pubs, at around fifteen, I was always the one who was calling for the next round, impatient that others were drinking too slowly.

There were a few incidents that now stand out for me when I think about how I may have been primed to be an alcoholic even before I 'decided' to become one.

At sixteen, I was able to hold more drink than most of my peers. But I remember one of my friends commenting to me that she didn't really like it when I had been drinking, because I seemed to change. I couldn't see it at all, but she said I could become quite aggressive. I'm not talking about physical fights here or anything like that; but it was as if alcohol changed me into someone else in a way that didn't happen to my friends.

There were some times around that age when I used alcohol completely inappropriately, even by a daft, young teenager's standards. I had a weekend job cleaning my friend's mother's house and once I turned up with a bottle of whisky to do it. There was nothing very sociable about that at all. I just decided that some alcohol would make the job more bearable. That's not a very healthy way of thinking and there were more times when similar things happened with drugs too.

I remember, one night I had an essay to finish for my English class and I was supposed to hand it in the next day but I hadn't even started it. So I decided to use some speed I had left over from my friend's birthday. I took that and stayed up the whole night writing. And yes, I was the sort of person who would buy my friends speed as a birthday present. Also, when I first started smoking dope, I quickly became someone who smoked dope rather than cigarettes. I had been a fairly heavy smoker from a young age – maybe another sign that I was bound headlong for addiction problems – but when I properly got into dope, that replaced cigarettes for me. I would roll up twenty joints every morning, put them in my cigarette packet, take them to college and smoke them throughout the day instead of regular cigarettes.

By the time I got to university, I sneered at all the students drinking their cider and experimenting with drugs, which a few of them did. It annoyed me when they could not handle their liquor and acted like giggling idiots, because I had got all of that out of my system at a younger age. In fact by the time I got to uni, I had already given up dope entirely. Of course by that age, I was ready to start going out with a drug dealer ten years older than me while my fellow students fooled around with each other, smoking a bit of weed and getting off with their classmates at happy hour down the student union. Even remembering those stories has made me smile wryly at how I ever denied that I had an 'addictive personality' when people would point it out to me. So even though I wasn't a proper addict by then and had no 'reason' to be, I guess it was in me all along. Can you relate to that, if you think about it in all honesty?

You may not have even got into drinking or drugs at a young age, but did you find that you acted differently from some of your friends? I have heard alcoholics and addicts recount how, when they look back, they were pretty much addicted to sugar and sweets as children. Another common theme seems to be feeling different from everyone else, almost like an outsider. Whatever your particular story, can you see that all along your reactions and behaviours might have been different from everybody else's?

The point of sharing all this with you is to show that sometimes we just are what we are and it isn't necessarily logical. If you can not put down the drink and drugs when your initial problems have vanished, don't waste your time trying to rationalise why you should be able to, why if you just try a bit harder, it should be possible. Just accept the facts as they are. You're an addict and you have to deal with it.

Another trap that many people fall into, trying to convince themselves that they are not really alcoholics or drug addicts, is believing that if *one thing* would change, then they would stop using. For example, they might believe that being stuck in an unhappy marriage, having a very stressful job, a toxic family, or little money, causes them to overindulge. Believe it or not, there are people with all of those problems who do *not* drink or drug over them.

Blaming other people, or negative circumstances, is a way for us not to have to look at ourselves. If you keep telling yourself that the other problems are the real issue, rather than your drinking or drugging, you are probably just fooling yourself. If you have identified with most of the other things I have already said, then that is almost certainly the case. And anyway, life will always be full of ups and downs, problems and situations over which we have no control. If you are truly an addict, you will just keep on justifying your using with new reasons when the old problems have vanished.

Not-that-bad-itis

There is a strange element to addiction, in that we often try to convince ourselves that we are not addicted. If you would like to try my controlled drinking experiment mentioned previously, then go ahead. You will soon find out if you are an alcoholic or not. If it is a severe effort, and you can not sustain controlled drinking for very long without reverting back to your old ways, then you are an alcoholic. I think hard drug users are less likely to believe that they do not have a problem, but it may happen in some cases.

What is common to both conditions, however, is the sense

that actually you are not that bad. I call this 'Not-that-bad-itis' as I believe it is a part of the illness. You may look at the man who is in and out of prison, or the woman who has lost her home and children, and think to yourself that you are not as bad as them. You haven't got into any serious trouble, so you can not have as much of a problem as they do.

There are three things that may have happened in cases where your addiction has not got you into any serious trouble. You have either been extremely lucky, or fought very hard to be a high-functioning addict, or these things have just not happened to you *yet*. The people you see on park benches, and in institutions, are people with the same problem as you, except that they are further down the line. If you are an addict, unless you have an unlimited supply of money and friends who will let you get away with whatever you want, and who will protect you no matter how obnoxious you become, these things *will* happen to you as you go further down the line of addiction.

The problems involved with addiction start off with small incidents like minor injuries, losing personal possessions, arguments with friends and family, inappropriate sexual behaviour and getting kicked out of bars and pubs. The middle-ground may be classed as drunk driving, broken relationships, illness, serious injuries, petty crime, and money problems. When you reach the end of the line, homelessness, mental institutions, prison, serious health problems and complete relationship breakdowns are some of the things you can expect. And of course we shouldn't leave out death, as that is the ultimate end if you can not find recovery. Whether through drunken accidents, organ failure or other health problems, untreated addiction can lead you to the grave in some very unpleasant ways. So if you have not had the misfortune to run the full spectrum of consequences yet, count yourself lucky; but know that if you were to continue, you would start ticking the boxes at some point.

Again there have been many people who have tried to disprove this theory and they have lost. Why wait and see? Why not get better now?

Other Notable Myths Busted

There was some plain old BS that I had to get straight with myself before I was finally ready to accept complete sobriety. Here are some other things that I had been lying to myself about, and the real truths that I discovered.

Alcohol does not work any longer – and it never will.

OK so I kind of understood that alcohol was not working for the moment, but I did not accept that it never would again. The reality is that when you have become an addict your neural pathways have changed – past a certain point, you are now an addict and your brain and body know it. There is nothing you can do to reason with it, or fight it. It just is. You will never get back to any time you used alcohol without any problems if you are now an addict.

36

This is also true of the fun you used to have drinking or taking drugs. You long for the days when it was romantic, fun and exciting. The truth is, it has not been like that for a long time – and it never will again.

In fact, quite a scary fact is that the more you go through withdrawals, the more dangerous they become. It is what is called the 'Kindling Effect'. Your body holds a memory of the last withdrawal, and so the next one will be even worse. This is how you know that your body takes your addiction seriously, and you should too.

You can not have just a few shots

Look plainly at the evidence here. I know that we tell ourselves time and time again that *this* time it will be different, but it never is for any addict. You are fighting against facts and reality if you believe you will ever be able to have a few drinks, or a few drugs, and be satisfied with that. Subconsciously, I knew I was lying to myself when I attempted to have a few shots, because I would always buy a litre of spirits 'just in case'. Just in case of what? Just in case I wasn't going to have just a few shots!

Drinking and taking drugs and dying misunderstood and wasted is not glamorous

I was never one of those people who thought I looked sophisticated with a nice glass of wine, but I almost gave up on sobriety a few times because I believed I was some tragic victim. It is actually not romantic or glamorous being a tragic victim – it is just tragic. Look at the reality and not the idea. Really, it's pitiful to be an addict in full flow. It's a horrible existence, not something to indulge in. I once got a friend of mine to video me in full withdrawal. Watching it played back made me cringe with shame, embarrassment and self-pity. Dying celebrating a life of recovery and happiness is a far better place to be.

I can live sober

I tried routes other than total abstinence for a long time, because I truly believed I would never be able to live sober or function like everyone else. Bear in mind that I had been an alcoholic all my adult life and barely drew a sober breath until my mid-twenties. I was convinced that there was no way I could live the rest of my life sober. Luckily I was wrong. Actually, everything that I have the capacity to do when drinking, I have the capacity to do sober. Some of those things are a little scary, but really it just takes a little courage to do it anyway. We are actually not a faint-hearted lot, us addicts. It is time to grasp the courage that you have shown just by surviving and use it to do new things sober.

I can cope with pain sober

This was really the crux of my inability to stop drinking – I was convinced that I would never, ever be able to stand the painful times without some kind of buffer or shield.

But actually, once you do it, you realise that nothing is the end of the world. Drinking and drugging, however, would certainly be the end of any hope for a normal or fulfilling life. Actually, in sobriety I have found that it is not necessary to hide or smother painful feelings. If you are having a tough time, it's OK to express it. Having a good old cry is not a sign of weakness – but giving in to your addiction is.

Even if things are painful, scary or otherwise troubling, drinking and drugging will never help. In fact pain will always pass. And if you are sober and clear-headed you can actually take action to solve problems. If you are hiding away in your addiction, you can not take steps to help yourself or to change the situation. You are simply hiding away, unable to do anything.

And if you are thinking that it is all very well for me to say this, but that *you* can not possibly cope with pain, let me tell you that I have Borderline Personality Disorder to contend with too. It's like emotional haemophilia, and pain feels magnified for people like me. But because I have taken steps to recover, I *can* live sober in even the direst of circumstances – and you can too. Can you think of any other myths you used to excuse your drinking? And do you want to junk them right now?

Honesty

Honesty is also a prerequisite for recovery, and for living healthily and happily. For myself, I was never in denial about my problem, nor about the extent of it. I always knew I was an alcoholic, although I didn't necessarily understand fully what that meant. But some addicts have been in denial for a long time about their problem and the chaos that their using has caused.

Many people want to blame everything else other than their drink or drug of choice for the problems in their lives. As I explained earlier, often people never attribute their problems to their using – they justify their drinking or drugging by pointing out all their problems and life circumstances.

While you may well have started drinking or using drugs because of your feelings or circumstances, in reality the problems you now face are more likely to be directly attributable to your using.

I am very sympathetic to your dilemma. I certainly started drinking because of an anxiety disorder that was no fault of my own. But, as my drinking continued, it caused more problems than it solved, and all the crazy things that were happening around me were almost all related to my use of alcohol, and the circumstances in which it landed me.

It was easy to carry on drinking, saying "Look at my life! Wouldn't you drink, too?" But the reality was that my depression was caused by my drinking; my homelessness was caused by my drinking; my relationship problems were caused by my drinking. In fact I would never have ended up in half the awful relationships I did if I had not been drunk all the time! I would have had more self-respect and love for myself as well as better judgement. Largely the problems in my life were perpetuated, not justified, by my drinking.

So I really want you to be willing to get honest about what drinking or taking drugs gives you.

I once made a list of what drinking gave me during binges and withdrawals – and here is an abbreviated version:

Physical Pain: Kidneys, liver, heartburn, shooting pains, stomach cramps, head feeling like it has been smashed in by a shovel, dizziness, bloody gums, dehydration, nausea, projectile vomiting, drunken injuries.

Ugliness: Swollen face, eyes, hands and feet, unable to wash, filthy, sweaty, stinky, greasy hair, dirty fingernails, bloated belly, bruises, furry teeth.

Wasted opportunities: Days in bed ill, unable to walk. Too dizzy to do anything. Missing out on fun, events, friends, socialising, sunshine, freedom.

Emotional pain: Massive anxiety for weeks after a binge, guilt, isolation, dread, shame, self-hatred, embarrassment, feeling vulnerable.

Miscellaneous: Spilt drinks, dirty house, cigarette burns everywhere, inappropriate behaviour, sneaking around, dangerous situations, wasted money, making promises I can't keep, recklessness, falling over, making other people angry, worried and stressed, major insomnia, afraid of the doorbell, risking my relationships, in and out of hospital, looking pathetic, being obnoxious, saying nasty things, loss of memory, letting people down, risking death, lack of judgement, losing things, not eating, missing work and appointments, drunken calls/texts/emails. Wasting my one precious life.

If you are totally honest, what does drinking alcohol or taking drugs give you?

Acceptance

Acceptance is such a crucial element of recovering from anything in life that it deserves a book all to itself. But as acceptance is a big part of recovery from addiction specifically, I felt its inclusion in this book was important.

There are all sorts of things that you will have to come to accept, not least of which is that you have a problem with drink or drugs - and will have to abstain from now on. We have touched on some of the other things that you will have to bring yourself to accept, and there will be more later on in this book.

But, for a moment, let us just look at what accepting means, and the power that it has in your recovery. If you can learn to accept certain things with grace, then you are in a very strong position to start your recovery from addiction. I happen to like the Serenity Prayer's use of the word acceptance: it talks about accepting the things you can not change. This is common sense really, and even though we know there is no point in moaning or worrying about things we have no power to change, many of us still spend our time fretting about them - which is crazy really, as it is a waste of time and energy.

Do you worry about what the weather was like yesterday? I guess not. It is not something you can change, so there is little point in dwelling on it. And actually there is no point worrying about what the weather will be like tomorrow either, because that is another thing over which you have no power.

It is fine to think about it, to plan and prepare, but other than doing that, why would you devote too much attention to it, as you can not do anything about it anyway. It would be far better to focus your energies on things that you do have some influence over.

There is a Buddhist practice I use and teach called Radical Acceptance. It is a very powerful tool that you can use to start accepting things from your past, present or future that you have no power to control.

Radical Acceptance is about letting go of worry, of judgement, of trying to fix things. It is not the same as complacency, but is a coming-to-terms with things that are going to be the way they are, no matter how we feel about them.

If worrying about some problem made any difference to the outcome of it, then I would say worry for all you are worth! The plain truth is that no amount of mental anguish you give yourself will be able to change history or the future, and so you are doing yourself a favour by letting all that tension go.

Acceptance is a big part of 'getting real' and is actually very liberating when you can master it. Imagine saving yourself all the time, bother and pain of focusing on things in a negative way when there is nothing you can do to change them anyhow.

Doing Radical Acceptance properly involves being so far removed from worrying about something that you do not even judge it as a good or bad thing – you just accept that it *is*. Some things for you to start practising acceptance on could be the fact that you may not be able to have things your way all the time. Sometimes you will just have to do what you have to do, even if you don't want to. And that could include things to do with your recovery.

For example, I know the last thing I wanted to do to get sober was to ask for help from anyone else, let alone to then accept that help. But when I realised, after a lot of painful trial and error, that I could not beat my addiction on my own, I knew I would have to accept the fact that I was going to need other people on my journey, at least to begin with; and I was going to need to set aside my pride and just get that help. And I was glad I did a few months down the line. And now I am eternally grateful that I did!

Other important things that you can learn to accept include other people and the things that they do. While we can all try to interact well with others and get on with them, ultimately you can not control what another person does or says, or how they react to you. I like to try and understand people, as this makes it easier for me to accept them and their behaviour. Again, this is not to say that you simply put up with being treated badly. If someone is not treating you well, then by all means talk to them and if they don't stop, then you have every right to exclude them from your life. But rather than doing that, a lot of us go down the route of trying to change people. While it is commendable to give people chances and advice, if they don't react well to these, then you just have to accept that you can not change them, and then let them get on with it – without you if necessary.

And last, but by no means least, you have to learn to accept yourself as you are, warts and all. When it comes to ourselves, we do actually have the power to change certain aspects of ourselves, such as the way we think and behave. But there are other things that we can never change, and we are wasting our time focusing on them in a negative way. Interestingly, it is actually easier to change those things we do not like about ourselves when we accept them. This sounds contradictory but actually it's not. For example, by accepting that I was an alcoholic, I was then able to push forward to becoming an alcoholic in recovery. That would never have happened if I had remained in denial about being an alcoholic for my entire life. I had similar challenges with accepting my diagnosis of Borderline Personality Disorder. I was diagnosed in my early twenties and I all but ignored it for the best part of a decade! By not accepting that I had the diagnosis, and that I was responsible for trying to manage it, I struggled with my resulting thoughts and behaviours for many years. It was only when it became too painful to deny it any longer that I accepted it and took on the responsibility of looking to find an effective treatment for it.

Again, I will never regret the day I accepted that this was a part of me, and that I needed to get help for it. I have successfully worked on it, and now it does not control my life in the same way that it did when I refused to accept it and left it untreated. So actually, acceptance gives you power, hope and a starting point for changing the things you can, as well as not dwelling on the things you can't.

Part Two

Get Held

Staying sober is not easy to begin with, but it is vital to maintain sobriety, despite the difficulties, in order to be able to work on your recovery. The second part of the Recovery Formula is for you to find a way to 'get held'. What I mean by that is that in early sobriety there will be a time, if not several times, before you reach recovery, where you just can not stand being sober any longer. You will want to jack it all in and head for the nearest off licence or dealer. If that never happens to you, at least in the first few months of sobriety, you're a better person than I am.

When you first get clean and sober, you will probably start to feel all sorts of confusing, and sometimes painful, feelings. You may feel guilty, regretful, depressed or even just bored. This will all stop when you recover. But you cannot have recovery without sobriety, so for the times when you want to reach for your substance, it is vital to have a support system in place.

The support system that individuals need will be different for everybody, and so will the length of time for which they are needed. But you would have to be one in a million if you did not need something, or someone, to help you through the early days.

In my experience, people who are in the same boat as you are the best support of all, and would always be the fail-safe that I recommend if asked for my opinion. But other people successfully use medication, counselling or other professional services to tide them over. Your pattern of drinking or drugging will help you to choose which method will best suit you. For example, I initially tried several unsuitable methods to tide me over, and if I had understood the pattern of my drinking, I probably would have changed methods sooner.

First, I tried calling my family whenever I felt like I was struggling, but that didn't work. Although I am lucky enough to have the most supportive parents on the planet, I felt guilt and shame for struggling when I had promised my family I was staying sober; and that only led to more drinking. I worried that I was worrying them, and that led me to drink, more often than not, before I could even pick up the phone. And then I would call them drunk, desperately trying to pretend I was not, which defeated the whole purpose anyway.

So then I tried Relapse Prevention groups, which were twice a week at my local alcohol service. They were very supportive, but they were only for an hour each time, so that didn't help me with my urges for the rest of the week.

By this point I had worked out that I needed support not just within working hours or once a week – I needed it at all times; because I drank on impulse, and when painful emotions rose within me – and I could never predict when that would happen.

So next I tried Antabuse, which if you have not come across it, is a medication that makes you extremely ill if you drink while taking it. When I mean ill, I mean it's time for hospital. It stays in your system for several days, so even if you miss taking it one day, you still can not drink for a few days after that. I thought it would help with my impulsiveness around drinking. I actually begged my alcohol worker to give it to me – it wasn't something that they gave to everybody because it is so dangerous if you drink alcohol while taking it. But that failed me as well, because I resented taking it and having nothing to comfort me when my emotions got too difficult to bear. I was on it for about a month. Then something happened in my life that upset me, so I stopped taking it for a few days. And I was back in the middle of another relapse before long, because medication did not hold me how I needed to be held.

The last thing I ever wanted to do, but the holding method which eventually saved me from relapsing, was going to Fellowship groups. At my first proper AA meeting I cried all the way through. Not because I was an alcoholic, but because I did not want to have to ask for help and to admit I needed other people. But everyone was very kind to me and as soon as I announced that I was new, I was supported, included and made to feel welcome.

49

AA was the perfect holding mechanism for me. Living in London, I could access it almost every hour of the day if I needed to. There were early morning meetings, late night meetings, meetings at weekends – and even when there was no meeting, I had a bunch of phone numbers from other members that I could call if I ever needed support.

And unlike the medication, AA gave me understanding, a feeling of belonging and some new sober friends to spend time with. I don't believe in God and I never did the steps, but it still worked to keep me sober while I did my own work on myself. And I figured out afterwards why it worked for me – my impulsive, emotional drinking meant I needed almost 24/7 support and my character meant I needed it from people who understood.

While my parents made themselves available to me on the phone whenever I needed, they are not addicts and so they found it difficult to understand what I was going through. The empathy shown from the other addicts was vital for me. I was not one of those people who found it easy to ask for help, but the beauty of Fellowship meetings was that you didn't need to say or do anything necessarily. My form of asking for help was turning up and having a chat with some people I knew, and sticking around afterwards to have coffee. Usually someone would ask me how I was doing, and if I needed to unload I could without fear of judgement.

If you are someone like I was – impulsive, emotionally fragile, and at risk of drinking or drugging at the drop of a hat, for any reason under the sun – Fellowship meetings could help you out. The other alternative to keep you safe might be rehab, especially if you lack the discipline to go to meetings or have other health care needs. Of course, there is no reason why you can't have more than one support mechanism.

So when choosing your holding method, really analyse your patterns of using drink or drugs. Do you think you need 24/7 support, or is once a week enough for you? Do you feel like medication would help, or do you need emotional support too? Would you prefer a professional to talk to, or people going through the same thing as you?

There is no right or wrong choice; there is only the right or wrong choice for you. You could well do what I did and learn the hard way what does, and doesn't, work for you, but you'd probably be better off looking at your drinking or drugging patterns first to understand which method would be most effective. It may even be a combination of some of the things above, or other things that you choose to put into place yourself. If you do happen to choose something that doesn't work, don't beat yourself up. Look at why it didn't work and start again. Do not give up on recovery entirely just because you hit a few snags. There will always be a way to get better that suits you. You may have to be a bit more open-minded and try different meetings or different services, but something *will* work for you if it fits in with your needs.

As for how long you will need this support system, well, everyone is different. Some people feel it is healthy to have fairly intense support forever, while others think it is only vital in early recovery. But one thing I will say is that there will most likely be what I call the 'jumping-off point' that occurs somewhere in your sobriety and you will need to make sure you use your holding mechanism a lot then.

If you've tried to go sober before and found that things were going alright until a certain point, you may already have encountered this jumping-off point. Anecdotally, I have heard it said that it is particularly common for addicts to relapse at three-month intervals. So, after three months, six months and nine months clean and sober, people seem to have particular difficulty in maintaining their sobriety.

My jumping-off points occurred at one month and three months. In my last year of struggling with staying sober, try as I might, I could never last beyond a month. Then when I finally made it to over a month, the three-month mark was extremely trying. At one point I had a bottle in my hand and was ready to drink it – but I saw sense and begrudgingly got myself to a Fellowship meeting, almost hoping it wouldn't work so I would be able to go home afterwards and drink. Fortunately for me, the meeting did work and I stayed sober another day. There were a few weeks afterwards where I was scared I would relapse almost every single day. That was my other big jumping-off point it seems. But I stayed sober anyway, because I was committed to doing whatever it took to stay sober, including using my support system to get me through. And I did make it through, because I wanted recovery so much.

Be aware of PAWS

There is a particularly good reason why your holding method is important early on and that is because of PAWS – or Post-acute Withdrawal Syndrome. Once you have got over the initial phase of acute withdrawal from alcohol or drugs, you will almost certainly be faced with a secondary withdrawal syndrome which can last for several months. It is caused by your body and brain trying to adjust to life without your substance and is nothing to worry about, although it can sometimes be unpleasant.

Physical symptoms of PAWS include:
Restless legs, insomnia, changes in appetite, nightmares, headaches, dizziness, poor co-ordination, poor reflexes, sugar cravings.

Cognitive symptoms of PAWS include:
Fuzzy thinking, confusion, racing thoughts, inability to solve problems, memory lapses, poor concentration.

Emotional symptoms of PAWS include:
Irritability, depression, over-sensitivity, anxiety, mood swings and, in some rare cases, suicidal thoughts.

The one thing to hang onto when you are going through PAWS, which tends to affect the majority of recovering addicts in one way or another, is that these symptoms will go away the longer you are abstinent. While you may find you are free of symptoms one day, and then suddenly they pop up again out of nowhere, their appearance will follow a downward trend.

It may be useful to think of these symptoms as signs that you are getting better and it can help to talk about them with someone you trust. If you really feel you can not cope with them, then contact a health care professional about the matter. If you are feeling suicidal, get help immediately.

But please remember, these symptoms are only a temporary condition and they will go away with time and abstinence – so just take care of yourself during this time and use your support system.

Feed your needs

In the early days especially, you must always make sure that you look after your basic needs. As addicts, we have been used to putting our substance of choice before anything, and everything, else. We may not have eaten or slept properly and we may have isolated ourselves from friends and family.

As human beings, we all have certain basic needs that should be taken care of if we are to function as happy, healthy people. So make sure you have all of these covered.

These include eating a decent diet, getting a good amount of rest and sleep, and having other people in our lives with whom we can interact and share our feelings. Although things like sleep may take some time to regulate if you are coming off drugs and alcohol, try your best to take care of yourself. Drink lots of water, exercise a bit, rest when you need to, and spend time with others. It is important not to isolate yourself, and to share your feelings with someone if you're going through a tough time. Of course having others to spend time with, and share happiness with too, is vital to being happy in the long-term.

Part Three

Get Committed

Don't even think about reading any more of this book until you have absolutely undoubtedly understood and implemented this step. Read it through thoroughly and decide that you are in this for the long-haul.

Alcoholism and drug addiction are unfortunately not light-hearted subjects. They are not problems that you can do a little work on and hope everything will just be alright. As I mentioned right at the beginning, addiction is a problem much, much bigger than you or I. It can end up taking over your entire life. Every single thought, every moment, every choice and every behaviour is influenced by your addiction. You have no life of your own – you are living through, and for, your addiction. That is how big addiction gets if it is left untreated.

And this is why a crucial step to take in order to conquer your addiction forever is to absolutely commit to beating it, come hell or high water. You need to be serious about dealing with this illness. You must always put your recovery first. And in early recovery, your sobriety must come above all else. Your friends, your family, your children, your job. Everything. After all, it is highly likely that you put alcohol or drugs before all of those things anyway, so why wouldn't you give the same commitment to your sobriety, and ultimately to your recovery? Why do you need to put it first all the time? Because without it, you would have none of those other things in future.

You will also have to commit strongly to doing work on yourself that may be difficult. Changing things about the way you think and do things is the root of recovery – and so you must commit to doing that work too.

Now total commitment will involve doing some things that you may find uncomfortable. But the alternative is not to recover and to continue to let your addiction run your life and possibly kill you.

Things like pride, fear and outside pressures may try to persuade you not to stay the course. Denial may even rear its sneaky head. But if you are ever to recover your life and start living rather than existing, these are things you must put up with and overcome – and you'll be extremely grateful and glad that you did.

When you are happily in recovery you will not need to use willpower not to drink or use, but in early sobriety, you have to be absolutely bloody-minded about staying clean and sober, no matter what. You need to be sober and keep a clear head in order to be able to work on yourself. But once that difficult period of pushing through is over, your recovery will mean that you won't be plagued by thoughts and urges to drink and take drugs. You may have the odd fleeting thought, but if you have strong recovery, it should be no more than that in the ordinary course of things.

But before you get to that stage, it is necessary to be prepared for some struggles. Cravings may beset you, difficult emotions may pop up and temptations will surely arise too. They may come out of nowhere and surprise you – so brace yourself and be prepared to maintain your commitment to yourself and your future. Recovery is worth it.

When things feel really bad, it may help you to see your recovery as a series of 'baby steps'. Every recovering addict has at least one day where they just want to give up and use. It is helpful in these instances to remember that cravings and emotions are fairly short-lived. Any time that you feel particularly pained by your experiences sober, commit to staying sober for just that day, or just that hour, or just that minute if that is what it takes. Have the good sense to realise that this emotion or craving will not last forever – it may be over within an hour, or twenty minutes, and will have more than likely passed by tomorrow. Use your support mechanisms when you feel like this. It is better to feel bad for a short while and get through it than to give up and use and go back into that whole cycle of guilt, shame and regret.

No-one ever regrets *not* caving in to a craving. Almost everyone is likely to feel awful the day after, if they give in to the craving and use. Both physically and emotionally you will be in a worse state than you were when you were just dealing with having the craving and the pain. Play the tape forward and recommit to your sobriety, even if you have to tell yourself that it is just for now. This is where your willpower will come into play. Just make it to the end of the day if you have to, and see how you feel the next day.

And please do not even think of using the excuse that addicts have no willpower – that is absolute nonsense. Think of all the times you fabricated, manipulated and pushed through just to get a drink or drug. How is it that even when we have no money and no friends, we still manage to procure our substance of choice by any means necessary? Addicts have a lot of willpower – we will go to the ends of the earth to keep drinking and drugging, to hide our problems and to protect our using. So I'm asking you to use that massive reserve of strength that you have to get you through the difficult early stages of sobriety.

I will give you some tips later on for staying the course. But for now, just know that if you can commit to staying sober early on and working on your recovery, the urge to use will go; you will be able to move on with your life – that is worth committing to for the meantime. Once you are past a certain point, there will be no more white-knuckling, no more nail-biting. You can just live your life as a fairly normal person when you're in recovery.

Recovery is possible – there is evidence out there of people who have done it and who feel grateful and happy now. I, for one, am one of those people. And don't believe that there is anything special about me. I have got sober twice and the first time I did it all wrong and relapsed constantly for a year or so. In my final year of drinking, I was in and out of hospital every other week, I had the local Mental Health Crisis Team and the Samaritans on speed-dial. I was having seizures and withdrawals and I even tried to take an overdose. I had a serious, serious problem. And sometimes I believed that I would never overcome it. But the one thing that kept me going throughout all the pain and illness was that I was committed to trying to recover.

I wish I had had a book like this back then, because my recovery was a lot of trial and many, many errors before I finally found the Formula. In a way, trying to recover was much more painful than just drinking. But when I look at the pain of trying to recover and the amazingly strong recovery and the wonderful life I have now, I can tell you I would have done the pain a hundred times over just to get what I have today. I really mean that.

Recovery is the most beautiful thing imaginable, and I actually think I am far more fortunate to be a recovered alcoholic than a person who never had any problems to begin with. That may sound crazy to someone who is not yet in recovery, but honestly it is the truth. The biggest storms create the brightest rainbows, so remember that when times get tough.

The rest of the Formula is designed to help make the process of maintaining sobriety and entering recovery easier for you, but without commitment all that would be meaningless. So decide today that you want recovery and that you want it with all your heart. And that you are willing to do whatever it takes to get it.

Become willing

The first requirement for anyone getting serious about their recovery, and not just their sobriety, is to become willing to do certain things. This includes a willingness to change, a willingness to be open-minded and a willingness to do things in a different way.

This is why you can not make someone stop drinking or taking drugs unless they absolutely want to. This is not to say that addicts can not be motivated to become willing. In fact, becoming totally honest about your drinking or drug use and the nature of your addiction, is often one of the steps towards willingness already taken. If you can see your addiction for what it really is, that is a great start to becoming willing.

And this willingness also means a willingness to take responsibility. As I mentioned before, I do not believe anyone is responsible for becoming an addict. Addiction is not caused by weakness of character; it is an illness. But everyone who has become an addict is responsible for becoming a sane and sober person.

No-one chooses to become an addict – we just get ill and there is little we can do about that. Sometimes we do not even see it coming until we are deep within the throes of addiction. But that is not to say that we should not accept responsibility for the consequences of our drinking or drugging. And it doesn't mean we shouldn't accept responsibility for our lives from here on in.

If you have come to the point where you know deep in your heart that you are an addict, or even if you do not wish to label yourself in that way, but you know you have some kind of serious problem with substances, you must take responsibility for turning your life around.

The reason for this is very simple – no-one else can do it for you. Other people can support and help you; this very book can help you. People can give you guidance and advice and tools, but there is only one person who can actually change your life and that is you.

I think a great many addicts dream of having a rescuer – someone who just swoops down and takes all our pain away. I certainly thought that way for a long time. I wanted someone to save me from myself. But the truth is that this is impossible. You are the only one who can make any real and sustained difference to your life, and for that to happen you have to become willing.

You will have to work at sobriety, and you will have to work at recovery, and you have to be willing to do that. The good news is that recovery really is worth it.

I will say it again: nothing worth having comes easily. But when you are committed to taking the road to recovery, and I mean 100 per cent committed, then recovery and a new, happy life is open to you.

When things are hard, it is vital to keep hold of that willingness and have faith that things will get better if you keep doing the right things.

Commitment and willingness means putting aside your pride and asking for help when necessary. It means having the courage to face challenges and fears. It means being patient and not picking up a drink or drug before you get to that wonderful place of recovery. It means allowing yourself to have faith that things can be different for you. It means trusting that the life you want is achievable and that you can get it if you work for it. And you can. No-one is hopeless and my own recovery from a seemingly hopeless mess has proved that.

Part Four

Get Replacements

Recovery is really all about replacement in lots of ways. And in your early sobriety, it is very important to replace a lot of the more tangible things in your life to enable you to stay sober. As you grow into recovery, you might consider adding some of these things back, but only if it is safe to do so.

The difficulty with addiction is that once we feel we have left it long behind, we are liable to become complacent about recovery. I hear stories all the time of people who managed to 'forget' they were addicts and then tried to use again; or who fall back into old patterns and behaviours, believing it will be alright.

One of the most frustrating things about addiction is surely that it is an illness of denial. Sometimes after a year or two sober, people start to believe that maybe one drink would be OK, or that seeing their old drug dealer socially would be alright. Recovered addicts sometimes consider themselves healed. And in a way they are, in that they no longer display the old behaviours related to addiction and they live happy and healthy lives for the most part.

But, if you are an addict, there is one thing that can never, and will never, change. You will never, ever be able to use substances again, no matter how 'well' you become. I would hope that when you find recovery and experience the wonderful joy it can bring you, you would not even want to go back to drinking or drugging. Being free from those things is liberating and amazing and I, for one, really do not feel like I am missing out at all by not having them in my life. But I will ensure that I never become complacent about remembering that I am an addict for as long as I live – that is the only way to stay safe.

So when it comes to early sobriety, there are several things you will need to replace, but let us start with the tangible things.

People, place and things

It is time to let go of all the triggers in your life and start living your life as if you were someone who does not have a problem with drink or drugs. I do not mean that you need to pretend you never had a problem, but I mean you need to put yourself inside the skin of a non-drinker or non-drugger.

So, would a teetotaller have a 'beloved' Jack Daniels T-shirt? Probably not. Would they have a whole array of different types of wine glasses, shot glasses, tankards and beermats? No, I don't think so. You need to get rid of anything that identifies you as someone who drinks too much or takes drugs.

Get rid of all your drinking and drug paraphernalia, whether it is directly associated to your substance or indirectly. You may think "What's wrong with having a Budweiser baseball cap or a commemorative pint glass?" Well, you need to start identifying as someone who is free from alcohol and drugs – and that means anything that is associated with them. Some of you may succeed with still having those things in your life, but really the only way to be safe is to be sure. If you are reluctant to get rid of any of these things, then it is a sign that you need to work on your willingness or your acceptance.

If you were a drinker, you may actually be surprised at the amount of drinking-related items you have managed to accumulate. I had alcohol-branded mugs, pens, T-shirts, calendars, shot glasses and key rings. I even had alcohol-related recipe books. That's not to mention the stash of pint glasses and ashtrays stolen from bars.

Once you have got rid of all the things that identify you as an active alcoholic or drug user, it is time to move onto the things that you will need to replace.

Places are one of the things that can often trigger people to relapse – and these often go hand in hand with certain people. I managed to get sober despite living with a heavy drinker at the time, and it can be done, but it is so much easier if you can distance yourself from people who are likely to trigger your using. My heavy-drinking boyfriend and I did eventually break up – and to be honest, I don't think we would ever have been happy spending the rest of our lives together, being on totally different pages with drinking and drug use. That is not to say that I would have been tempted – in fact his getting wasted all the time put me off both drinking and him. But we had different interests when I sobered up and eventually we would have grown apart anyway. So if your current partner is still using drugs or drinking, while it is up to you what you do about that relationship, it might be worth thinking about it in the grand scheme of things and whether it will last.

The same rule goes for friends of yours. Luckily, I had already got rid of most of the hard-drinking people from my life, but there were still a few in my phone book that I would have happily got wasted with. If part of your ritual of drinking or drug-taking was to hang out with certain people who encouraged or enabled your using, then it may be time to leave these people behind. I would say that this is even more crucial for drug users than it is for drinkers. I personally do not know anyone who has given up drugs who still hangs out with the same circle of friends. The reason for this is probably obvious. Drinking socially can be done by people who do not have a problem with it and many of your friends may be normal people who enjoy a beer or a glass of wine. Using drugs really moves into a much greyer area, as drug use is far less accepted socially, and so it is more likely to be done in an underground way, with certain types of people you probably don't want in your life any longer. Needless to say, you will need to block or delete the phone number of your old dealer if you happen to be a drug user trying to get clean.

Lots of us who have gone most of the way down with drinking or drugs have found ourselves hanging out in some pretty grotty places. Was there a bar you went to that you wouldn't be seen dead in if you weren't a heavy drinker? Or was there a real classic 'alkie' pub where you used to go? I had one of those – it was my local for years. No-one there really noticed I had a problem, because quite frankly most people there had a problem!

A lot of people ask me whether I think that if you are an alcoholic you should never go into pubs. I am lucky enough that I have never had a problem going into pubs, probably because towards the end of my drinking, I was fairly safe in pubs. Hanging out in my bedroom was where I did most of my drinking. What I would say is that early sobriety is about keeping safe and if you are worried that you might feel tempted, just don't go.

Remember, your sobriety is number one from now on, and that takes precedence over celebrating friends' birthdays, watching the football down the pub and anything else that involves being around people drinking or taking drugs. If you are the slightest bit concerned that you may be tempted or feel uncomfortable, then it is best not to go. Many people in recovery find that later on going down the pub sometimes is not a problem, but they end up going far less often than they used to anyway.

A special note for the drug users here – watch yourself around drinking and pubs. A lot of people giving up an addiction tend to become cross-addicted to something else. I see it all the time with alcoholics getting addicted to sugar and caffeine. So if you are a drug user, it is really important to watch out that you do not become addicted to alcohol! That would be just as bad for you as your old habit. A lot of ex-drug addicts find that they benefit by becoming teetotal too, although this is something you will have to decide on for yourself. As always, it is better to be safe rather than sorry. If you think drinking is becoming a problem, too, then it is.

Now here is where we move onto the replacement side of the equation. Just because you do not choose to drink or do drugs any longer, does that mean that you shouldn't have friends or that you shouldn't socialise? Does it mean that you have to isolate yourself and never have any fun? Of course it doesn't. It means that you have to find new things to do, new friends to see and new places to go. Sometimes we may have left behind old friends who it might be nice to have back in our lives – you know those people you left behind because they disapproved of your lifestyle or who couldn't bear to be around you because of your using? Maybe it is time to see if they might want to become a part of your life again. Or you could start investigating new people, activities and places to go.

This is not only a nice thing to do but it is actually a vital part of early sobriety and recovery. A lot of relapses happen due to people isolating themselves or becoming bored. Isolation is unhealthy. If you are alone with your thoughts sometimes that can become dangerous in early sobriety. You may be tempted back into old ways of thinking and old patterns of behaviour, or you might start feeling sorry for yourself – and that is a very quick way to relapse. It is far better, and a lot more fun, to start doing new and interesting things.

When people get clean and sober they are often amazed at all the free time they have, now that they are not chasing around after drink and drugs or obsessing about procuring their substance of choice. What a great opportunity to use all that time to find something you really love doing, or to see people you really enjoy hanging out with. It would be great to start socialising with sober people – or at least people whose lives do not revolve around drinking. And there are plenty of places where you can meet these sorts of people. The internet is responsible for opening up a whole world of opportunities to us, from meet-up groups to forums, where we can find people with similar interests and lifestyles. And, of course, to find other people in recovery. Communities of people devoted to recovery are springing up all the time.

The mainstays of your social life could be meeting people for coffee, tea, lunch or dinner or doing activities. Going to exhibitions, art galleries or the theatre, getting involved in culture. There are so many fun and interesting ways to spend your time.

And what about hobbies and other ways to enjoy your life? I hate the word 'pastime' because I believe the things that you do should not just be ways to 'pass the time', but

71

things that you love doing. Is there something you have always wanted to do? A class you could join? Something you always wanted to learn? Do you want to travel, to help others, to get re-educated, to start a business, to take up a sport? There are so many ways to enjoy a new, sober life – and plenty of people to hang out with who enjoy being sober as much as you will.

Replacing Behaviours

An absolutely vital part of starting to recover is to replace your behaviours with healthier ones. We have already looked at changing the things in your life to suit your new identity. Changing your behaviours is all about that too.

I have seen people get clean and sober while still doing some dodgy things, but the more of your unhealthy behaviours that you can replace, the happier you will be.

Firstly the most important behaviour to replace is around your using. You will need to act in a new way when triggers come up. It sounds really obvious, but it is actually a little more complicated than it sounds because this is where individuals will vary.

Replace your 'Trigger Behaviours'

You may know this as identifying triggers, but there is a little more to it than just that. In a nutshell, there will be certain patterns to your using that will show up time and time again, and you will need to replace the way you react to these triggers with different behaviours. It is also important to try to eradicate or minimise these triggers as much as humanly possible. It is especially important to do this in early sobriety in order to prevent relapse.

For me, I drank when I was emotional. Full stop. But for some people, they drink or want to take drugs when they are bored, angry, lonely, tired, under stress or pressure. You will need to find ways to take yourself out of those situations that trigger you, and also ways to cope with unavoidable situations in new ways.

While no-one can necessarily avoid the various emotions of everyday life entirely, it was important for me to be able to avoid chaotic occurrences, which tended to trigger massive emotional states.

So, for example, in my relationships, I had to make clear what was acceptable and unacceptable to me. I had to speak out about upsetting occurrences rather than bottling them up inside, ready to explode.

So if you have similar issues, you must work on making your life as free of those occurrences as you can, especially early on. This might mean avoiding certain people, places and things as I mentioned previously. Or it might mean learning to adapt your life to get rid of those unhealthy triggers. For example, you can not expect to avoid stress if you are a stockbroker and you can not avoid being triggered by boredom if you sit around watching TV all day. You can not expect to lead a quiet and peaceful life if your partner is a drama queen and you will never be able to avoid the volcano of rage if you bottle things up and do not talk about them. It is important to build a sustainable life which caters for your particular needs to be fulfilled and your triggers to be avoided.

Secondly, I had to do something different when I was actually upset. As I said, life is unpredictable and we never know when we will feel the trigger being pushed despite our best efforts to lead good and suitable lives. Some of these will be short-term solutions and others will be longer term.

So for me, instead of drinking, when the emotions hit hard I would go out for a long walk or share in an AA meeting. Or if I was particularly angry, then I would call my mum to rant and rave, or I would have a session on my punch-bag. These all helped in the short-term.

In the long-term, to deal with emotions, I used NLP and DBT skills, which is what I now use to help my clients. When I felt angry, I would talk about what was making me angry with the person concerned; I would be assertive and ask to get my needs met, or at least understood. I focused on doing what was effective as a solution, rather than being driven to poor reactions by my emotions. Other people may do the steps prescribed by Fellowships to keep them behaving in healthy ways.

So, when do you feel like using most of all? Do you use on impulse, or can you clearly see particular patterns? What are your triggers? How could you remove some of them from your life? And how will you cope in the short-term and the long-tern when your triggers hit you hard? It is important to plan for these occasions so you will know what to try when you feel at your worst. Think seriously about this, as the solution is unlikely to come to you when you feel on the verge of a relapse.

Replace what your substance gives you

There is an apt metaphor that I want to introduce here. Have you ever tried to take a teddy-bear away from a small child? It can not be done without a lot of kicking, screaming, trauma and upset. Unless, you take that teddy-bear away and replace it with something else. If you try to take the teddy-bear away and hand the child a lollipop, you are much more likely to be successful than if you just snatch the toy away and leave them with nothing.

Equally, you can not take the teddy-bear away and expect the child to be happy if you replace it with a stick of celery or a book on applied mathematics. The replacement 'thing' has to be equally valuable to the child, and it has to do the same thing or something better than the original teddy-bear.

Some of what I said earlier about finding new and fun things to do will apply here, but we have to go a little deeper than that. So you have to be prepared to really look at what alcohol or drugs gave you. And this may involve peeling back a few layers until you get to the crux of the matter.

Ask yourself the question: "What stops you giving up alcohol/drugs?" And then when you have your answer to that, then ask the further question "What do you want instead (of that)?" and then continue with "What stops you (doing that)?"

Ask these questions in alternate ways until you feel that you have reached the real answers. It would be helpful to do this with a Recovery Coach, so that you don't stop too early and arrive at a superficial answer. Sometimes it can be very painful to realise the real reason why we drink, so I would definitely recommend doing this with someone else, preferably a professional.

Here is an example of the questioning in action:

What stops you giving up alcohol?

    A. I am afraid I won't be able to cope.

What do you want instead?

    A. I want to be able to cope.

What stops you being able to cope?

    A. I don't believe I have the resources.

What do you want instead?

    A. I want to have healthy coping strategies.

What stops you having healthy coping strategies?

    A. I have never known how to comfort myself.

What do you want instead?

    A. Comfort - and knowing how to get it from myself.

This was my own pattern of drinking and the reason that I used alcohol above all else. Once I had identified that I was a comfort drinker, and that I usually drank to comfort myself, I knew that I had to replace that comfort with something else – a different teddy-bear. So from there on in, I made it my mission to learn other coping strategies and healthier ways of bringing myself comfort.

There may be only one main reason why you drink or take drugs, or there may be several. They may come down to questions of identity, the past, limiting beliefs about yourself or unhelpful thoughts. Whatever they are, if you can learn new ways of giving yourself what drink or drugs gave you, this is a massive step towards recovery.

I should point out that it is clearly important that the new things you do are healthy! If you purely drank to find oblivion, you will probably find that it goes a little deeper than that. There will be some healing that needs to be done around the reason you do not like reality. The answer clearly isn't to top yourself or to sleep all the time. The answer will be something to do with changing your thinking about life and healing old wounds so that you no longer seek oblivion.

Secondary gains

A very important but often-missed aspect of what your addiction gives you is that the actual state of being addicted does give you some advantages. Hard-won and ill-gotten advantages, but advantages nonetheless.

It may be even more difficult to admit to, or accept, these secondary gains than it is to admit you have a problem, but please be open-minded about it. A lot of people refuse to get better because they will be missing out on all the secondary benefits that having an addiction gives them. They may not even understand it in those terms, but if you find that you are falling off the wagon despite addressing every other aspect of your addiction, then you will need to consider if there may be a deeper reason behind you perpetuating your problem.

For example, for some people, having a problem makes them feel special. It sounds crazy to fulfil that need by having an addiction, but it is one of the things that we human beings can do without being aware of it. These secondary gains are usually hidden very deep in our subconscious and we may be unaware that we have been fulfilling them via our addiction.

It is like the lady who overeats because she is scared of being hurt by men, so she subconsciously tries to make herself unattractive to them by becoming obese. Or the agoraphobic who maintains their anxiety because deep down they are afraid of being who they are and asserting themselves in the world. Or the man who stays depressed his entire life because it means he gets attention from his long-suffering wife and doesn't have to go out to work. All of this may be processed at a totally unconscious level, so it is nothing to feel bad about if you have remained trapped in your problem because of secondary gains, but it is something worth looking at.

So think about what having your addiction might have given you in terms of secondary benefits. Did it protect you in some way from other people? Did it keep you safe? Did it ensure you got attention? Did it mean your partner had to look after you? Was it a way of attracting a care-giver? Did it mean you never had to take any responsibility? Did it mask a fear of failure, or a fear of success? Did it give you certainty – being stuck in the same old patterns? Did it make you feel accepted by other people similar to you? Was it to show people how much they hurt you? Either people from the past, or those in your life now? Was it a way of crying out for love?

When you have found out your secondary gains, the tactic that I find most useful in challenging your behaviour in relation to them is simply to turn them on their head and to realise how ineffective your addiction was as a strategy. And of course to look for other, healthier strategies to give you the same end result; or even to come to an understanding that you do not even need the so-called secondary gains in your life.

For example, if your addiction was in some way a strategy to get your partner to look after you, it was a pretty poor strategy, because all the time you were risking having your partner leave you for good, as your behaviour upset them more and more. If you were always putting your addiction to drink or drugs before them, then you were at very real risk of losing them totally.

If your need is to be looked after and loved, then there are much better ways of achieving that than hurting yourself and others. Being yourself, and being kind to others, will attract people to you who will love you and care for you, without you needing to act out to get it.

Going through secondary gains can be a painful, if enlightening, process. No-one likes to discover how they have been sabotaging themselves when all they wanted was to be protected, loved or listened to. It may be worth going through any issues with a Recovery Coach, a counsellor or a therapist if you think that you have identified some complex ones that may be holding you back from recovering.

Changing your thinking

Replacing your old, screwy ways of thinking with healthy and positive new ones is the most important replacement of all. This is another subject that deserves a book all to itself. And I have written one for you, should you choose to use it. *The Happy Addict* takes you on a journey through all the sorts of changes that you will need to make to your thinking in order to become recovered and happy.

But as I have pointed out throughout this book, there are many methods you can use to change your thinking. Some find doing the 'Twelve Steps' prescribed by Fellowships useful, others will prefer to follow a book – and some people will want to do both.

I can not stress enough how important it is to make some kind of changes to your thinking. This is the final step in recovery, and the piece of the puzzle that takes you from merely being sober to being absolutely recovered, and to your never needing a drug or a drink again.

You will have to change the way you think about yourself and others, replacing negative ways of thinking, being and behaving with more positive ways. If you don't make the changes, then you don't want recovery enough. And I am sure that is not true of you.

Adopt a new attitude

You will never change and rebuild your life if you are someone who insists on looking at the negative side of things, because you will never be open enough to see opportunities. Negative thinkers are notoriously rigid, and in order to change, you need to be flexible. If you are someone who is used to 'black-and-white thinking' you need to open yourself up to the grey areas. If you don't think that's true, consider what got you to the painful place you are now in. It wasn't your life events or your problems – it was your reaction to them and your thinking about them.

I first got into trouble with my drinking because I had a crippling anxiety disorder and I used alcohol to mask that. I am not going to beat myself up about the fact that I chose that route, because it was all I knew how to do at the time to stop the pain and to function. But I absolutely recognise that it was not a smart move in the grand scheme of things, and that my reaction to my problem (ie. alcoholic drinking) was responsible for the life of chaos and complications that ensued.

So, above all, work on changing your reactions to things, and on building a positive mind-set and attitude. This is the final key to recovery. If you do not do this final part of the Formula, you will be in for a life of white-knuckle sobriety. Not using, but not better. Clean, but not changed. Sober, but not happy. It is not a fun place to be. It is far better to put the time and effort into cementing your sobriety with healthy thinking, because that is when you will find recovery. And that is when your life will begin again.

On the next page you will find a quick run-down of the most helpful attitudes you should work on cultivating to give you healthy thinking and to make your recovery a strong and happy one.

Beth's Top Attitude Tips:

- Accept things you can not change
- Focus on the positives in every event
- Look at what you can learn from problems
- Realise that you are responsible for sorting your life out
- Remain objective and do what is effective, rather than acting on emotions
- Breathe and think before you react
- Cultivate willingness and have an open mind
- Learn to be understanding, patient and kind
- Stop being stubborn and getting stuck – instead become determined to change!
- Do the next right thing
- Be honest
- Have integrity – only do things that give you a clear conscience
- Forgive yourself and other people
- Build your great qualities and work on eliminating your weaknesses
- Check that you are living according to good values
- Keep the end in mind whenever you do anything – ask yourself: will this help me achieve recovery and happiness?

Summary

I wrote this book because I am an addict and I spent most of my adult life searching for the solutions to my problems.

It was a very painful and frustrating journey, as there was no road map that I could find, and every mile seemed to be a full of obstacles and pitfalls.

Although I felt like giving up over and over again, I am so glad that I didn't; not only because I am extremely happy and grateful to be in recovery now, but because my own journey, my mistakes and my victories can help you.

I believe that through my own experience, and talking to many other addicts, I have identified a logical framework within which alcoholics and drug addicts can work towards, achieve, and maintain recovery.

While the Recovery Formula as set out in this book is universal and essential for all who want to recover from addiction, how you achieve recovery in terms of practical help will be different for everybody.

Some will need more support than others, some will need professional help to address long-standing mental health issues, and some will benefit from specialist treatments and services. But I know that you will be able to find recovery just as many others have, by using the Formula set out in this book and using it to choose the appropriate treatment methods for you.

Get Real

The honesty about, and acceptance of, your problem of addiction is ultimately down to you. You can prevaricate, disguise, justify, hide and lie to yourself all you want, but one day you will know the truth. My hope is that the recognition will come sooner rather than later, as it will save you a great deal of pain and suffering. Life is short and precious, and the sooner you start living it the better.

Get Held

To be able to benefit from the help that is available to deal with the core issues that fuel your addiction, you need to be clean and sober, otherwise treatments can not work. I can not say how long this 'holding period' needs to be, as it will depend on the individual. But it is self-evident that there must be a period of sobriety, so that help can kick in.

In my case, I found that an understanding Fellowship of other addicts was the answer. I found a place where I could be totally honest, confident in the knowledge that they understood. Just realising that it was not just me was very liberating. No shame, no apologies; just cups of tea, understanding and occasional hugs.

Those moments of doubt and weakness in early recovery can be overcome by knowing that you have your own support mechanism, whether it is people, medication, or a combination of both. You must find something that will hold you how you need to be held, to keep you strong and supported during your early recovery.

Get Committed

Easy to say, not so easy to do, but sobriety and recovery need to come first in your life if you are to succeed. You have to be totally serious about your recovery, willing to seek help and to change.

You did not choose to be an addict, but you are one, and it is your responsibility to deal with it, because only *you* can. If you commit to changing, sobriety and recovery are achievable. You have to be totally single-minded, and even somewhat selfish, in pursuit of your goal.

All I can say to you, to comfort you when times are hard, is that recovery is the best thing I have ever done, and I am not alone in saying that. There are many of us who have recovered and now live happy lives.

I know it is hard – I have been exactly where you are. And I recovered. I have my life back – even more than that, I have a wonderful life now that I am proud of and enjoy. It will be the same for you, if you just have faith and make the commitment.

Get Replacements

Replacing people, places and things are all part of avoiding relapse and creating a new life. The key, that moves you into a world where you never feel the need to drink or drug again, is replacing behaviours and patterns of thinking that led you to pick up the bottle or chase the elusive dragon.

It is in these areas that you might need professional help. If you have a skewed way of thinking, or problems with emotional regulation, as I had, there are some techniques available that can help you better manage your life, and avoid the triggers that caused some of your problems. Most addicts have hidden traumas that must be addressed.

Neuro-linguistic Programming and Dialectical Behaviour Therapy may not be terms with which you are familiar, but to me they were literally life savers. And they are part of the toolkit with which I personally help other addicts to get well.

There are many different treatments that can help you to make these vital, fundamental changes, including rehab centres, day programmes, Twelve-Step programmes, CBT and other therapies.

Whichever treatment you choose, you must understand that the goal is to heal old wounds and change your thinking, so that you can be healthier, happier and start living your life for you, rather than being a slave to addiction.

Conclusion

Get Real, Get Held, Get Committed to your recovery and Get Replacements for all that bad stuff in your life and in your head. In that way, you really can become the person you were always meant to be.

One final point to make is that addicts can be vulnerable to relapsing when they least expect it. Sometimes after a long period of sobriety, that addict voice will pop up, seemingly out of nowhere, telling us it might be a good idea to drink or use. Be ready to meet it.

Check in with yourself regularly and analyse how you're feeling. Are you overly stressed, isolated, tired, uneasy, lonely, run-down or sad? That is the time to touch base with whatever methods worked for you to keep you sober, or to look at adding more to your program of recovery. Relapse tends to creep up on us, but we can prevent it by remaining mindful of how we're feeling and taking steps to address any triggers or troubling moods.

We can never afford to get complacent about recovery - it should always remain the Number One commitment in our lives, even after years of sobriety - because without it, we would have nothing else. You may have less intensive work to do later down the line, but you should never stop building on and developing your recovery so that you can remain clean, sober and happy for the rest of your life.

I wish you every joy and happiness in your sobriety and your recovery. You can do it!

Afterword

I will just make a special appeal to people who have recovered and are trying to help others to find recovery. Often, when we are in recovery, we want others to find the happiness and joy that we now have, and it is tempting to try and foist your own treatment methods upon them. I appreciate that you want to help them to find happiness too, but insisting on them doing things your way is not the best way to help people.

If Fellowship groups have helped you, don't start shoving AA or NA down other people's throats – they won't thank you for it and it will not help them much. In fact they may resent you for it. Don't go around telling people that certain treatment models, rehabs or medications are the only way to recover. Give them this book instead, and then let *them* work out how they can apply the Recovery Formula to their own life to make it work for them.

If others approach you afterwards and ask you how you found your recovery, then by all means share with them what worked for you. But I firmly believe that people recover best and fastest when they have education about their problem, a deep understanding and a choice.

Hopefully this book will give them all that. Pass it on.

Glossary

AA	Alcoholics Anonymous
CBT	Cognitive Behaviour Therapy
DBT	Dialectical Behaviour Therapy
Fellowships	Twelve-step groups, such as AA and NA
NA	Narcotics Anonymous
NLP	Neuro-linguistic Programming

18759187R00058

Printed in Great Britain
by Amazon